this is my faith

Sikhism

by David Dalton

BARRON'S

First edition for the United States, its territories and dependencies, Canada,
and the Philippine Republic published in 2006 by Barron's Educational Series, Inc.

© Copyright 2006 by ticktock Entertainment Ltd.

First published in Great Britain in 2006 by ticktock Media Ltd.,
Unit 2, Orchard Business Centre, North Farm Road, Tunbridge Wells, Kent, TN2 3XF

All inquiries should be addressed to:
Barron's Educational Series, Inc.
250 Wireless Boulevard
Hauppauge, NY 11788
www.barronseduc.com

ISBN-13: 978-0-7641-5968-8 (Hardcover)
ISBN-10: 0-7641-5968-2 (Hardcover)

ISBN-13: 978-0-7641-3477-7 (Paperback)
ISBN-10: 0-7641-3477-9 (Paperback)

Library of Congress Control Number: 2005939049

Picture credits
t = top, b = bottom, c = center, l = left, r = right,
OFC = outside front cover, OBC = outside back cover

Alamy: 7b, 9c, 9b, 11c, 13t, 13c, 14b, 17c, 19t, 21b, 23t, 27c. Art Directors and Trip Photo Library: 12b, 13b, 27b. Corbis: 11b,
19b, 23c, 23b, 25t, 26, 28b. Plan U.K. and Plan International: OFC, 1, 2, 4b, 5all, 6, 7t, 8, 12t, 16, 17b, 18, 20, 21t, 21c, 22t,
24t, 26t, OBC. World Religions PL/Christine Osborne: 7c, 9t, 11t, 15b, 17t, 19c, 22, 24b, 27t, 29t.

Every effort has been made to trace the copyright holders, and we apologize in advance for any unintentional omissions.
We would be pleased to insert the appropriate acknowledgments in any subsequent edition of this book.

Printed in China
9 8 7 6 5 4 3 2 1

Contents

Words that appear in **bold** are explained in the glossary.

I am a Sikh

"My name is Inderjeet Singh. I am 13 years old, and I live in a small village in the Punjab, in India. I am a **Sikh**."

"The word 'Sikh' in the **Punjabi** language means 'disciple.' Sikhs are the **disciples** of God who follow the writings and teachings of the ten Sikh **Gurus**."

This is Inderjeet. Sikhism teaches him that all people are equal. This means that Sikhs treat men and women, and people of different faiths, in the same way.

All Sikh men and boys wear a turban on their heads and have Singh as part of their names.

"Being a Sikh is important in every part of my life; in what I believe, how I behave, how I look, and even in my name."

"I say prayers every day. These are from the Guru's teachings. I also read from the **Guru Granth Sahib**, our special book, every day."

Reading the writings of the Gurus helps Inderjeet to learn about how he should live.

The special Khanda symbol is shown on the Sikh flag and is often used to decorate turbans.

"The **Khanda symbol** is very special to the Sikhs. It is the double-edged sword of life surrounded by the circle of **eternity**."

5

My family

"I live with my mother, two brothers, and two sisters. My father is dead. We say he left us to be with God."

"My home is small. We have three little rooms, which is enough for all of us."

Inderjeet's father was called Manjeet Singh. His mother's name is Amarjeet Kaur.

Inderjeet's mother and his sister have their own names and also the name Kaur.

"When girls are **confirmed**, they are given the extra name Kaur, which means 'princess.' Boys are given the name Singh, which means 'lion.'"

"Parents often help their children to learn about Sikhism by telling them stories of the Gurus. The stories teach us to be proud of our beliefs."

Children are taught the stories of the Gurus at home and at school.

A typical Sikh meal is a type of bread called roti and different vegetable curries. Men and women cook and share all household jobs.

"We help our mother around the house by doing the housework. Then we help her to prepare the family meals."

What I believe

"Sikhs try to follow the teachings of the Guru Granth Sahib. This is the work of our Sikh Gurus, or holy teachers, which teaches us how to live and behave."

"A holy man called Guru Nanak was told by God to teach people a new religion in which everyone was treated the same."

Inderjeet enjoys reading about the lives of the Gurus. The stories are a good example for him to follow and are very interesting.

Guru Nanak was born in 1469. His family believed in the Hindu religion, but Guru Nanak chose to start a new religion called Sikhism.

"The first Sikh teacher was Guru Nanak. He taught that there is only one God and that everyone is equal."

"Guru Nanak traveled around telling people about Sikhism and teaching them to treat all people with kindness. An early follower was Bhai Lalo, a carpenter."

Nanak stayed in the simple home of Bhai Lalo. Nanak liked it better than the homes of the rich because Bhai had earned his money honestly by hard work.

The Gurmukhi script was developed by Guru Angad so that he could write down Guru Nanak's teachings. Gurmukhi means "the mouth of the Guru."

"When Nanak died, Guru Angad became the leader of Sikhism. He improved the **Gurmukhi script** and collected the writings of Guru Nanak."

9

LEARN MORE: What is Sikhism?

- Sikhism began in 1499 in the Punjab, in northwest India. There are over 25 million Sikhs living in India today. Most Sikhs live in the Punjab region. Sikhism is the world's fifth most popular religion.

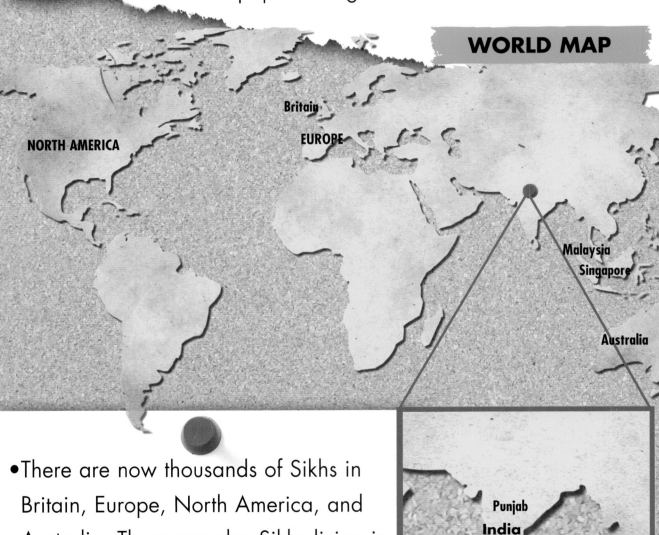

WORLD MAP

Britain

NORTH AMERICA

EUROPE

Malaysia
Singapore

Australia

Punjab
India

- There are now thousands of Sikhs in Britain, Europe, North America, and Australia. There are also Sikhs living in many other parts of the world, such as Malaysia and Singapore.

One of the Panj Pyare pours **amrit** into the hands of Guru Gobind Singh as part of the confirmation. This is to show that the Guru is equal with the people that follow him, although he is a leader.

- Guru Gobind Singh founded the **Khalsa**, which started with five men who said that they were willing to die for their faith. These men are known as the **Panj Pyare**, or "the five beloved ones." The Panj Pyare formed the first Khalsa with the Guru.

- Sikhs worship in a temple called a **gurdwara**. Most gurdwaras have a prayer hall where the holy book, the Guru Granth Sahib, is kept.

Each gurdwara has a **langar** hall. This is a room where everyone gathers after the gurdwara service to share a meal. Langar means "shared food."

The other Gurus

"Each of the Gurus gave us teachings to follow. Guru Arjun and Guru Teg Bahadur died for their faith."

"Some of the Gurus were forced to fight to protect **Hindus** and other Sikhs from the cruelty of rulers who wanted everyone to change their faith to **Islam**."

Har Krishan was known as the Child Guru. He was only five years old when he became a Guru. He died of smallpox when he was eight years old.

12

Guru Gobind Singh was a skilled horseman, archer, and hunter. He is usually shown with a falcon, a hunting bird.

"I am really interested in Guru Gobind Singh who gave his life fighting for the Sikhs. He was very brave. I read about him in the books at school."

"Guru Ram Das built Amritsar, which is the holy city of the Sikhs. He also wrote a hymn that is sung at Sikh weddings."

Amritsar was a forest before Guru Ram Das started to build the lake there which now surrounds the Golden Temple.

When the Golden Temple was finished, Guru Arjan Dev put the first copy of the Guru Granth Sahib inside the temple.

"Guru Arjan Dev was the son of Guru Ram Das. He built the beautiful Golden Temple on the lake in Amritsar, in India."

13

LEARN MORE: A special book

- The Sikh holy book is called Guru Granth Sahib. It contains hymns and teachings written by the Gurus and other holy men.

- When the tenth Guru, Gobind Singh, died in 1708, he said that Sikhs did not need a living Guru, but that the Guru Granth Sahib should be their Guru.

The Guru Granth Sahib is written in a script called Gurmukhi.

These children are learning to read Gurmukhi in a gurdwara school.

- This symbol is known as **Ik Onkar**. It means "there is only one God." These are the first words of the Sikh holy book.

The Ik Onkar symbol is often used to decorate Sikh objects.

People who look after the Guru Granth Sahib and read it out loud in the gurdwara are known as **granthi**.

- The Guru Granth Sahib is kept on a raised place called a **manji** in the main hall of the gurdwara. It is kept there so that everyone can see it and read it.

- When it is not in use, the Guru Granth Sahib may be covered by a cloth called a rumalla. Women as well as men can be a granthi, or reader.

The woman at the back of this picture is holding a fan called a chor. It is waved over the Guru Granth Sahib as a sign of respect.

The Five Ks

"Sikhs who are part of the Khalsa wear five symbols of their faith. These are called the **Five Ks**, because each begins with the letter K in the Punjabi language."

"Kesh is the word for long, uncut hair and a beard. As Sikhs we do not cut our hair. We keep it tidy by tying it up in a turban, or **patka**."

Inderjeet keeps his hair tied up in a patka. He wears a turban for special occasions.

The kangha is a wooden comb used by Sikhs to keep their hair tidy. It is a symbol of cleanliness.

"We comb our hair with a kangha. We also wear special cotton shorts called kacha, which are comfortable to wear."

"The kirpan is a short sword. It is a symbol of the fight against evil and for truth."

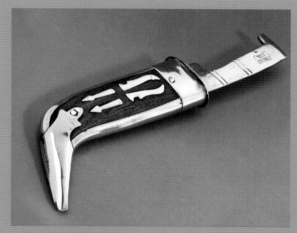

Today the kirpan is worn as a symbol to show that Sikhs are prepared to fight for the beliefs of the poor and weak.

This Sikh wears the kara and carries a kirpan across his shoulder.

"The kara is a steel bangle that Sikhs wear all the time. It reminds us to do the right things the Gurus taught us."

Why Sikhs wear turbans

"Sikh men never cut their hair or beards, because this is what the Guru Gobind Singh asked. He said that we should wear turbans to keep our long hair tidy and safe."

"When we wear a turban, we are showing our love for God and that we are happy to be Sikhs."

Inderjeet can tie the turban himself, but his mother often helps him. It takes time and practice to do it well.

Very young boys and girls wear a piece of cloth, called a patka, tied around their hair until they are old enough to wear a turban.

"Turbans come in every color and pattern. But the most commonly worn are white, deep blue, and orange."

"There are many different ways to tie a turban. Men keep their hair inside by tying it into a top knot or making it into a plait."

Many Sikhs wear a patka under their turbans.

Some Sikh women wear a turban and a scarf to keep their hair tidy and to stay cool in the hot weather.

"Most women just tie their hair back in a bun. They cover their hair with a scarf when they visit the gurdwara as a sign of respect."

Where I worship

"Sikhs can pray anywhere at any time, but the place where a lot of Sikhs gather to pray is called a gurdwara, which means Guru's door."

"We take our shoes off, and wash our hands and feet before we enter the gurdwara. This is to keep the gurdwara clean and as a sign of respect."

Sikhs put their hands together, bow their heads, and close their eyes when they pray. This is so they can concentrate on the prayers and God.

At the end of the service, the Guru Granth Sahib is opened anywhere. The words on that page are read out, there is a blessing, and the service is finished.

"There is a gurdwara at my school, which I visit every day. There are services throughout the day. I go in and stay for as long as I can before lessons."

"Everyone sits cross-legged on the floor of the gurdwara. This is to show that we are all equal."

We make sure that we don't point our feet toward the Guru Granth Sahib.

Everyone gives something to the langar meal. They can bring food to cook, give money, or help to prepare and serve the meal.

"At the end of the service everyone goes to the langar hall to share a meal. People from all religions can join in the service and share the meal."

Special festivals

"One of our most important festivals is **Baisakhi.** This is the day that we remember when the Khalsa was created and when the Sikhs were given the Five Ks which has become our uniform."

"Baisakhi takes place in April, and is also part of the harvest festival when we celebrate the gathering of new crops."

During Baisakhi, langar food is served in the streets.

Traditional folk dances from the Punjab, called the Gidda and Bhangra, are performed during the Baisakhi celebrations.

"At Baisakhi, we visit gurdwaras and listen to readings from the Guru Granth Sahib. Many people decorate their houses with flowers."

"Sikhs also celebrate **Diwali**. This is when we remember the release of Guru Hargobind from the Muslims. Lamps are lit outside the gurdwaras and we are given sweets."

The biggest Diwali celebration takes place at the Golden Temple in Amritsar, which is lit up with thousands of lights.

During Hola Mahalla the Sikhs give displays of horseriding and swordsmanship.

"**Hola Mahalla** is a festival when Sikhs show off their fighting skills. There is a parade and mock battles. Afterwards, we have music and poetry competitions."

Gurpurb festivals

"We have many festivals when we remember times in the Gurus' lives. These festivals are called Gurpurbs and often there is a procession when the Guru Granth Sahib is carried through the streets for everyone to see."

"The most important Gurpurbs are the birthdays of Guru Nanak and Guru Gobind Singh and the deaths of Guru Arjan and Guru Teg Bahadur."

Gurpurb celebrations begin with a reading of the Guru Granth Sahib by a group of granthi. They read the Guru Granth Sahib nonstop, from beginning to end, which takes forty-eight hours.

These Sikhs are performing Gatka, a type of Sikh **martial art**, during a procession to celebrate Guru Nanak's birthday in India. The celebrations can last for up to three days.

"During the gurpurbs, there are parades through the streets and special displays. Many gurdwaras are decorated with flags and flowers, and some are lit up with candles and lights. We have a special service with hymns and prayers. After the prayers, Karah Parasaad is served. This is a sweet-tasting food that has been blessed."

Special occasions

"We have lots of special ceremonies to mark important times in our lives. In many families, when a boy reaches a certain age, he goes to the gurdwara and his first turban is tied on by the granthi."

"For me, the most important ceremony was my confirmation, or amrit, when I became a Khalsa."

During the amrit ceremony, the person drinks the amrit, or holy nectar, five times and has some sprinkled on his hair and eyes.

The amrit is stirred by Sikhs who are acting out the parts of the Panj Pyare.

"For the confirmation ceremony, the amrit is prepared. A bowl is filled with water, and sugar is added while prayers are said."

"During a wedding ceremony, the groom wears a scarf called a palla. The bride holds one end and the bridegroom holds the other end to show their **unity**."

At the ceremony the couple sits in front of the Guru Granth Sahib and the granthi explains the duties of married life.

Friends and family sing hymns around the coffin before the body is taken to be cremated.

"When someone dies, we believe that his or her soul leaves the body. The body is usually **cremated**, and the ashes are put into the river."

LEARN MORE: Holy places

- Sikhs visit historical places to remind themselves of important events in the lives of the Sikh Gurus.

- One of the most important places for Sikhs is the Hari Mandir, or Golden Temple, in the city of Amritsar in Punjab, northwest India. Thousands of people visit the temple every day.

The Hari Mandir, or Golden Temple, in Amritsar. The name Hari Mandir means "eternal throne."

The house where Guru Nanak was born. On one side of the house there is now a gurdwara called "Nankana Sahib."

- Guru Nanak, the founder of Sikhism, was born in the western Punjab, not far from Lahore, Pakistan.

Guru Gobind Singh lived in Anandpur, in India, for nearly 25 years, and the Anandpur Sahib gurdwara attracts thousands of visitors.

- The Anandpur Sahib gurdwara was built on the place where Guru Govind Singh gave amrit to the first five Sikhs and started the Khalsa. Anandpur is also known as the Holy City of Bliss.

Glossary

Ik Onkar.

Amrit Sweetened holy water, used during the confirmation ceremony.

Baisakhi A festival to celebrate the creation of the Khalsa. It is sometimes spelled Vaiskahi.

Confirmation A ceremony which means that a Sikh is now a full member of the Sikh faith.

Cremated When a dead person's body is burned.

Disciples People who follow the teachings of a leader.

Diwali The Hindu festival of lights is also celebrated by Sikhs. Also spelled Divali.

Eternity Lasting for ever and ever, never ending.

Five Ks All Sikhs have to wear five items, known as the Five Ks (because they all begin with the letter "k"), at all times. Kesh – long hair; kangha – a comb; kacha – cotton shorts; kirpan – a short sword; kara – a steel bangle.

Granthi Someone who looks after the Guru Granth Sahib and reads it out loud in the gurdwara.

Gurdwara This word means "Guru's door." A gurdwara is where Sikhs worship, and is also the place where the Guru Granth Sahib is kept.

Gurmukhi Script This is a type of writing used for the Guru Granth Sahib. It was composed by Guru Angad.

Gurus This word means "teacher." For Sikhs, the word means the first ten leaders of their faith.

Guru Granth Sahib The holy book of the Sikhs. "Granth" is Punjabi for book and "Sahib" means master in the Hindu language.

Hindu People who follow Hinduism, the ancient religion of India. Sikhism has some ideas that are similar to Hinduism.

Khanda symbol.

A kangha (comb) and kara (a steel bangle) – two of the Five Ks.

Hola Mahalla

This festival was first started by Guru Gobind Singh as a day for Sikhs to practice their fighting skills and to hold mock battles.

Ik Onkar This means "there is only one God." These are the first words of the Guru Granth Sahib.

Islam The religion based on the teachings of the Prophet Muhammad. Its followers are called Muslims.

Khalsa People who have been confirmed as full members of the Sikh religion and who wear the Five Ks.

Khanda Symbol This is sign that has a special meaning for Sikhs and which appears on all Sikh flags. It is made up of four weapons used by Sikhs at the time of Guru Govind Singh.

Langar A shared vegetarian meal, which is prepared after every Sikh service by volunteers.

Manji The "throne," or special place, for the Guru Granth Sahib in the gurdwara.

Martial art A way of defending yourself if you are attacked.

Panj Pyare This means "the five beloved ones." These are the five men who joined the first Khalsa with Guru Gobind Singh in 1699.

Patka The cloth young Sikh boys wear to cover their hair.

Punjabi The language spoken in the Punjab in India.

Sikh The word Sikh means "a learner or disciple." A Sikh is a believer in Sikhism, the religion founded by Guru Nanak in 1499.

Smallpox A disease that killed many people in the past.

Unity Being joined together as one.

Index